For Patty Brulotte -
Thank you for all
the help with our move
~ Bob Jacob

THE DAY

SEAMUS HEANEY

KISSED MY CHEEK

IN DUBLIN

✪ The Outstanding Author Series

#6 *The Day Seamus Heaney Kissed My Cheek In Dublin*
#5 *How In The Morning*, by Chuck Miller
#4 *The Casting Of Bells*, by Jaroslav Seifert, Nobel Laureate
#3 *The Farm In Calabria*, by David Ray
#2 *The Poem You Asked For*, by Marianne Wolfe
#1 o.o.p.

✪ The Editor's Choice Series

Editor's Choice IV: Essays from the U.S. Small Press
edited by Fred Chappell (forthcoming)

Editor's Choice III: Fiction, Poetry & Art from the U.S. Small Press
edited by Morty Sklar

Editor's Choice II: Fiction, Poetry & Art from the U.S. Small Press
edited by Morty Sklar & Mary Biggs

Editor's Choice: Literature & Graphics from the U.S. Small Press
edited by Morty Sklar & Jim Mulac

✪ The Ethnic Diversity Series

#5 *Patchwork Of Dreams: Voices from the Heart of the New America*
edited by Morty Sklar & Joseph Barbato (stories, poems, essays)

#4 *Speak To Me: Swedish-language Women Poets*
edited & translated by Lennart Bruce & Sonja Bruce

#3 *Eight Days: An Elegy for Thomas Masaryk*, by Jaroslav Seifert
Czech & English; translated by Tom O'Grady & Paul Jagasich

#2 *Mozart In Prague: Thirteen Rondels*, by Jaroslav Seifert
Czech & English; translated by Tom O'Grady & Paul Jagasich

#1 *The Casting Of Bells*, by Jaroslav Seifert
translated by Tom O'Grady & Paul Jagasich

✪ For a complete booklist or catalog, write to us:

The Spirit That Moves Us Press
P.O. Box 720820
Jackson Heights, NY 11372-0820
(718) 426-8788

THE DAY
SEAMUS HEANEY
KISSED MY CHEEK
IN DUBLIN

by **Bob Jacob**

poems 1986-1999

Number 6 of The Outstanding Author Series

The Spirit That Moves Us Press
Jackson Heights, Queens
New York City —— 2000

"The Visit" first appeared in a special issue of *The Café Review* that was dedicated to Donald Hall. "Luck" first appeared in *U.S. 1.*

Design, layout and typesetting by Morty Sklar.

Grateful acknowledgement is made to Peter and Dorothy Rinaldo, Norma Vogel and Barbara Yates for cash contributions to the press, and to Marcela Bruno for technical consultation.

This first edition is published in September 2000 in paperback and hardback bindings, twenty-six of which are signed and lettered A-Z.

Number 6 of the Outstanding Author Series; Also issued as Volume 13 of *The Spirit That Moves Us.*

The Spirit That Moves Us (ISSN 0364-4014) is indexed in *Index to Amercan Periodical Verse; Poetry Index Annual; Short Story Index; The American Humanities Index; Granger's Index to Poetry; M.L.A. International Bibliography.*

Printed on acid-free paper with soy-based ink.

Library of Congress Cataloging-in-Publication Data

Jacob, Bob, 1932-
    The day Seamus Heaney kissed my cheek in Dublin : poems, 1986-1999 / by Bob Jacob.
    p. cm.–(Number 6 of The outstanding author series)
    "Also issued as volume 13 of The spirit that moves us"–T.p. verso.
    ISBN 0-930370-53-8 (hard cover)–ISBN 0-930370-52-X (paper)–ISBN 0-930370-54-6 (signed A-Z)
    I. Title. II. Outstanding author series ; no. 6.

PS3560.A2478 D38 2000
811'.54–dc21

                                                99-052547

For my wife, Betty

The Poems

Everybody Says Hello

Face white as her hair,
my mother mumbled
"everybody says hello."
I leaned forward
to make sure of the words.
The oxygen mask had slipped
and I wanted to adjust it.
Again, "everybody says hello."
Eyes closed, only her lips moved.

Once Aunt Floss
laughed so hard she peed her pants.
Uncle Johnny didn't think it was funny.
He was a very proper man.
Always a shirt and tie.
Very proper, until a fourth beer
slurred him into the picture.

When uncle Jimmy finally
stopped chasing fire engines
he married a fiery burlesque queen.
A ghastly blow to the family.
She turned out to be pure sugar.
Give you the shirt off her back.
When she was a bar-maid
she'd give me a pickled egg and beer.
Ten years old, I'd sit at the bar.
"For God's sake Bobby
don't tell your mother."
My mission was a pail of beer

for the old man.
A lovely trip home
thanks to aunt Grace.

When I was small
my grandfather would drop
his uppers while talking
just to give us a laugh.
A straight laced man.
Didn't drink, smoke or swear.
Stood out from the rest of the family.
His second marriage
was to a lady who loved me
but didn't like Catholics
so she didn't attend my wedding.
That was her loss, and
I loved her just the same.
A tough old bird who died of cancer.
Never heard her complain.
Shrivelled down in the corner of a couch,
she told me about being in Canada
selling real estate, driving a car, smoking,
when ladies didn't do those things.

Uncle Harrison was five feet one inch.
Introverted, shy, always broke,
borrowing money from the family.
Aunt Catherine's death broke him.
Most thought him removed from the world,
disappearing and reappearing

like a magician's rabbit.
He was kind to me though.
We worked Karp's Candy Store together
one very long hot summer.
He handled the tables. I had the fountain.
He taught me how to professionally
gift wrap a box of candy.
We'd sing while we mopped the tile floor
every night after closing.
We're still not sure when he met his maker.

Sometimes when the trees out back
talk to one another
and the sky rumbles just before rain,
I'll stand at the window and listen.
Sometimes, everybody says hello.

The Visit

for Donald Hall

The house wanders through add-ons
in abrupt rights and lefts,
through tilting broad paneled doorways,
into hallways and rooms
and then a stairway from out of nowhere,
skinny the way they used to make them,
leaning just a bit to the right,
the banister smooth, still solid.

He is ahead of me talking about books
that line walls in makeshift shelving,
or look up from half-filled cartons
that touch my legs like word brush.
All the time slanted wide floor boards
moan their hello, tired from the weight
of books in every corner of every room,
or is it his relatives of four generations
trying to comfort him in his losses,
first his mother, then his mother-in-law, then Jane?

Now he is lying full length on an old couch,
his arm lackadaisical over an easy chair.
He is having an occasional back spasm,
nothing serious he says, but flat is better.
Gussie, his dog, brings in one of Jane's slippers,
lays it at my feet, tail wagging.
He says Gussie still thinks she is coming home.

The tv is on with the Patriots playing,
only his big dish antenna is broken
so he asks how I like his herring-bone tv picture.
We laugh while his old khaki pants and slippers
get up slowly to see a young couple at the door
who thought they ran over his cat last week.
While he is outside Gussie is nervous
knowing when they took Jane the last time
she didn't come back.

Stretched out again he is much taller
than I thought.
While the tv gasps in the background
he begins a monologue of grief so deep
my insides cry when he
has trouble speaking of his wishes
for her last hours and minutes
to have been different.
He says, I was out of town when I called
and she told me of the sudden nosebleeds.
He says, I shuddered and for no reason
I know of, thought, my God she has Leukemia.

Now the warmth of this old farmhouse seeps in
as he speaks intimately of their love,
which kindles in me a desire for my own wife,
a desire for all lovers to be together.

He can barely whisper the words, and even
Gussie's head seems to bow in sad remembrance.
Suddenly he is up in spite of the back
asking if I would like to see Jane's wall,
a wall filled with photos of
her sad beauty looking at us,
or sometimes the two of them in embrace.

Later we drive a few short miles to her grave.
It is a very old New Hampshire cemetery
with leaning weathered stones
of relatives and farmer families.
Toward the rear looking through trees at a lake
a modern darkly polished stone stands,
whose choice, he says, perplexed him until
he realized it duplicated the Vietnam Memorial.
Two names on the stone—hers, 1947-1995;
his, 1928-, and her words spoken to him:
I BELIEVE IN THE MIRACLES OF ART BUT WHAT
    PRODIGY WILL KEEP YOU SAFE BESIDE ME

The Day Seamus Heaney
Kissed My Cheek In Dublin

Years ago a bright spot
was a wizened old Irish lady
with a heart of fire,
who visited my mother every Friday,
her thoughts and experience
zeroed in on reading tea leaves
in an eighty year old brogue
so thick you could lean on it,
which my brother and I did,
laughing as we switched cups
giving her the same leaves
to read over and over,
rejoicing at the different readings,
all a positive look
into a future of endless possibilities

as though she were glimpsing
the day when Seamus Heaney
would arrive sending sparks
through our class at University College,
critiquing and offering encouragement,
gently pushing our mix of ages,
to help words sing
as his quiet voice seemed to,
causing the air to turn green
with his personal melody
until the class was ended
and half of us rushed away,
while he stood off to one side alone,

and I thought what the hell,
said "Seamus, how does a pint sound?"
His immediate smile provided the answer,
and actually more than one pint
entertained us in O'Dwyer's Pub
until he suggested a walk
and an early supper of Fish and Chips,
his Irish purse at the ready.

So we ambled in the green air,
along a narrow canal,
he in deep thought,
we respecting his time,
when to our delight a bench appeared
and we sat, Seamus on my right,
another on my left,
three standing behind,
the youngest fiddling with my camera
while I gauged the poet's mood,
which seemed anything but tragic,
so I said
"wouldn't it make a great picture
if you kissed my cheek
(his arm already lay across my shoulders)?"
A look of wary concern seeped to his brow,
forcing a loud guffaw
and slap of my own knee,
when suddenly the kiss was planted
loosing his own raucous laughter.

Of course the young student
missed the shot,
but in retrospect a photo would never have caught
the peals of memory
that play in my mind to this day.
And so my friends,
what I learned that day is
that this poet's poet is a wildflower
with a humor that slides
from his eyes and mouth simultaneously.
Wherever you are Seamus,
I'm raising one to you
at this very moment.

Some Days

are like this
waking tired
the pills for poison ivy
have me so
jazzed up and jumpy
sleep barely comes
after multiple fantasies
and conversations
with the past and present
but dawn does arrive
and the day begins
with small errands
all aimed
around our house guest
and our planned visit
to the Ivoryton Playhouse
a matinee at 2:30 P.M.

and I'm thinking
the sky is gray
my brain is gray
and heavy clouds
proclaim rain to come
but off we go early
to find a tea room
our friend has read about
in Higganum
which it turns out
can't be found at first
until an elderly lady

gray and quiet
offers to lead us
just a few miles she says.
I am watching the time
as always
but she is good on her word.
Mrs. Fuller leads us along
back roads through
heavy wet green
stops gets out
leans into our
car window with her
aged cloudy eyes
points out the entrance
as she continues to
talk as I glimpse the time
she telling us
the area's story, her story
how last week
she almost died in a hospital,
and I begin to admire
her gentle bearing
her need for company
but the clock is ticking
as I slowly slowly pull away
thank you   thank you

The tea room is closed.
The green shrubbery seems
to rear up in defiance

and the sky leans on us
as we continue our journey
to pick up our tickets
and begin another story
of finding lunch
which we do finally
and it's time for the play.

The ladies to the ladies' room
and I to an attractive forty-ish
woman usher who has
what appears to be
a small flower petal
in her bouffant hair
   me: let me get that for you
   she: oh thank you
but it isn't a petal
rather, a small silver label
that says 'made in China'
   me: it seems you were
made in China
   she: blushes and giggles
   me: well perhaps we
shouldn't go into that
   she: puts her hand on my arm
and says "you devil you"
so I sit and

for the first time think perhaps
things are picking up
and I notice
that the audience
is speaking in old murmurs
so many haloed heads
senior citizens everywhere
and then a light tap
on my shoulder
penetrating old eyes
and a quavering voice
asks if my name is Stuart
and I say no
is yours Isabelle
but instantly regretting
the old face scrunched up in concern
   she: no but you look like Stuart
   me: no my name is Bob
   she: oh the resemblance
is so strong
   me: Stuart must be very handsome
   she, serious: oh yes he was
a very handsome man
and my day jumps
another notch
while the lights fade
and the play "Sylvia"
by A. R. Gurney begins
a story about life

as seen by a dog
played very effectively
by a beautiful young woman
who at one point
begins to sing the old song
"Every Time We Say Goodbye."
I cry a little
and the other two actors
join her in the words
a trio in lament
making their way
in a hard business
suddenly bringing all
the family and friends lost,
home in my throat and eyes
when the actress
playing the dog jumps
into the prissy
visiting lady's lap
licking and sniffing her,
the lady screaming
the audience howling
with laughter
and I finally realize
that today
we are to cry
laugh and just be

Bernie

He is eighty-four.
  He is legally blind.
He is on dialysis.
  He is in pajamas.
He is eloquent.
  He is in love.
The bedroom is small.

  The cross with Jesus
  over his bed, large.
We meet for the first time
offering life stories.

  I represent a church he
  attended for fifty years.
I read from the book of Revelation
and the prophet Daniel.

  His clouded eyes stare at my voice
  as I share some positive poems.
He likes poetry, he says
"Wrote some to my wife in the '40s."

  He says "I am having a love affair."
  This stops me cold.
"After fifty-five years I'm not married anymore."
I am silent on the edge of the chair.

He senses this and smiles.
He says "My wife has Alzheimer's.

She is back in our courting days.
I really have to mind my manners."

He takes me into the next room,
introduces me to his wife and her caretaker.

Later when I am leaving
the last thing I see is Bernie

holding her hand, saying
"You look so beautiful today Anne."

She smiles at her boyfriend.

Twilight

Twilight comes quietly
to Peck's Lake,
where many purples
rest beneath light fog,
where today's almost-caught fish
becomes tomorrow's hope,
and far off voices
slide clearly across water.

Tonight
a ten-year-old in bare feet
executing an occasional plié
at the end of our rented dock
holds lightly in her hand
a shining, shimmering flute.
We, her father and I,
carrying a bit of vodka
and much love inside
sit on an overlooking porch
suggesting her favorite tunes.
She is in no rush,
milking, as it were, the moment.
She is trying to visualize notes.
The silvered flute
slowly comes to her lips
as the program begins.

Lake ripples move toward her,
their dark hollows listening intently;
swallows swoop in conductor arcs
as even her two brothers fall silent.

Lean On Me

for Charles A. Brown
1930-1951

After a night of wind,
twigs and branches
litter the driveway.
Bending to the largest,
I toss it into the woods,
it lands upright
against a rhododendron
leaning, resting actually,
as though the night
has taken too much
and now this bush
pillows its exhaustion,
its loss of place
as we all feel it.
If he knew
how he would go
Charley would have laughed
at the idea of
a swarm of Chinese
blowing bugles up a hill
and he might have said
yeah—and they will be
playing Stardust
while I dance with
Joan Leslie,
her tits piercing my heart.
while leaning against
a handball wall

an ever present toothpick
dangling from his lips,
everything in sight
fiercely familiar.

Two Former Players Of The Ozone Park Braves Meet On Liberty Avenue Under The El Outside O'Hagen's Bar

Billy Pierson's eyes were different.
They looked hurt without a bruise.
The smoothest lefty off the mound
was nervous and twitchy.
He said "Charley caught it
at the Chosin Reservoir.
We became separated just after arriving.
He was assigned to a forward position.
When the Chinks came it was like
a swarm of ants with flags and blaring bugles.
It was awful, just awful.
I got out in the retreat.
It was really bad, really bad."
I offered to buy him a beer.
He said "no, I gotta keep movin',
gotta keep movin'."
We shook hands and said goodbye.
Never saw him again.

I can still see and hear Charlie
inching a lead off of third base,
hands cupping his mouth,
a bow-legged foghorn.
"C'mon Jake, give us a hit,
give us a hit.
Send me home now,
send me home."

The Baker

Around a gentle curve
sunken bread slices
stand on a sloped hill.
Loaves of them separately staggered,
each inscribed to be eaten
by time, and those below them
old dough planted deep.
When the baker calls all will rise.

Korea

a Visit

The crosses walk to me over rolling hills,
their arms reaching out,
memories and my friends in their midst.

Where is the sound of Chinese bugles
on a cold crinkled morning?

Where are the swooping hills, brief sparks on their sides
knocking my friends down?

Where is the world where fingers claw at snow
for greater depth to cover fright?

Where is the feeling upon returning home
that people will never understand or even care to?

A bird flies overhead landing among the rows.

The breeze this morning brushes leaves gently.

I kneel and pray they were greeted so.

The Poem

for Terry

There is a point where
love and friendship intermingle
especially when a friend is so sick
he stumbles as he kisses
your cheek hello and you
return it to skin that feels
paper thin, all the time
trying not to hug him
too hard because of his pain
and thinking now about his
struggling to get out of a chair,
body slow, disjointed
like a puppet's
all because of two new
cysts and the additional radiation.
As you talk to him
understanding that his conversation
sometimes matches his hallucinations
because of the heavy narcotic doses,
knowing he is seeing someone
sitting next to you when
no one is there,
his eyes so heavy-lidded
fighting a hollow cheeked fatigue
—that doesn't stop him
from asking for your opinion
of a poem he is writing about death.

Stoop Ball

First you need the air
that young boys breathe.
Then a Spaldeen
with its exceptional bounce,
and of course a street with
trees to help deflect
a really long hit
but with enough openings
for an occasional home run.
The boys must learn
to take a deep breath
just before throwing the ball
at a brick stoop with
at least three steps.

One boy per team,
who, while pitching
on any given day
may be Freddie Fitzsimmons,
Don Newcomb, Hugh Casey,
Ralph Branca or Preacher Roe.
While in the field maybe
Pete Reiser or Dixie Walker.

The rules must be clear.
A ball caught on a fly is an out.
A ball going through legs
into the street is a single.
A double is a ball landing
on a fly in the street
before the large tar patch.
A triple is over the patch,

and a home run is all the way
to the opposite sidewalk.

An occasional car
coming down the street
is all right, but a
careful watch is essential.
Each boy must take sharp
aim at the very edge of
a step, throwing the ball
with all his might,
hoping to hit an edge
to give the ball loft
and distance
into home run land.
Such a hit is rare
and should be marveled at.

Not really necessary, but
intriguing is a door at the
top of the stoop with
small panes of glass.
The boys should be prepared
to chip in and pay
for a pane now and then.

If, after reading this
you have any questions
about this serious, but fun sport,
wish your way back to Queens, N.Y.
in the 1940s, and watch.

Understanding

On line in the bookstore
a woman with a baby in her arms
I say *how old*
she replies *five weeks*
I say *one forgets how small they are*
she replies *he never takes his eyes off of me.*
I think, if my next meal were you
I wouldn't take my eyes off you either.
Suddenly a small girl around seven years old,
her arms wrapped around four books
bumps my leg for attention.
Aha I think, the sister.
She has no front teeth, and startling blue eyes.
She says *he cries all the time*
I reply *well babies do that*
she says *it's okay*
'cause I understand him

My Son At Twenty-three

You take a step
each time we meet,
a step ahead
as I retreat
into a cloud
of love for you,
quite beyond
the child I knew.

It's pride I think
that takes me there,
and the willingness
of each to share,
in many ways
not father/son,
it's as though
we've just begun.

Luck

It's as if the steep hill
behind our house
wants to fall in our direction
only some lucky force holds it back.
It is so cold
the trees cackle at the situation
as rocks poking through snow
look at rabbit tracks just outside the door.

Last Fall
we dug a horseshoe swale
to run snow melt in a luckier direction.
One of the few times
we saw bad luck coming.

When our daughters were younger
I laughingly told them,
if you want good luck
keep your knees together.
Twelve grandchildren later
we all smile lucky smiles.

A lucky rabbit's foot always struck me sad,
a creature's luck having run out to make it.
It feels good to see this morning's rabbit
sitting like a rock
thinking he's lucky we can't see him.

World War II

Queens, N.Y.C.

There weren't many cars
—gas was short—but
the few that traveled
had the upper part
of their headlights
painted black
turning them into monsters
with heavy eyelids
in case of an air raid,
which we practiced for,
only at our age we weren't
sure it was practice
and when the sirens sounded
their basso profundo
would wailfully ascend
the scale to high soprano
and then down again
in numbered waves
and when the count
was right my father
would grab his flashlight
white civil defense helmet
with red white and blue
circular insignia on it
rushing onto our block
yelling lights out in his loud
Air Raid Warden's voice
banging on doors so
the German bombs

wouldn't find us
huddled under the
dining room table
where we sought safety,
and on occasion
searchlights would roam
the sky lighting our
young fear of possible harm
which never came
and then one day
a boy with straight brown hair
sat behind me in class
and asked my name
in an English accent
his being Alan White
so we became friends
as he slowly
over many months
told me his
war orphan story
and how the bombs
we were fearing
had landed on
his house instead.

Just So You'll Know

for Emma Regina Bour

When I was a small boy
my parents would walk me
over warm cement sidewalks
in Queens, New York City,
to a place called Forest Park,
a refuge of sorts, away from
train and traffic noise,
to a special boating pond
where children would sail
toy boats of all sizes.
Some boats tied to a string
were walked around pond's edge,
but I always pushed my boat outward
to catch a breeze across the sea.

Yesterday at seven weeks old,
you lay cradled in the crook of
my left arm, where I cradled
that small boat.
Your entire body fit along
my forearm, with your
bootied feet cupped in my hand.
Like a sail catching wind
your arms and hands fluttered,
and I gazed closely at your perfect
infant features, at your fingers
the length of my thumb's width.

And like my sailboat, when
I finally release you
to begin your own voyage,
and when the breeze
of your breath one day ceases,
I will be there to gather you in.

The Leaf

Walking in deep woods
with friends,
looking for blackberries,
laughing, kidding
one another,
trying to outpick
each other
—even as the sun
sprinkles us
through the trees
we spray each other
with thoughts
of children and their
children who are probably
playing as we are
with friends,
and like us searching
for common ground,
rubbing elbows,
trying not to be pricked
by blackberry bush stickers,
and resolved
to leave some berries
for deer and bear,
letting civilization
recede to the point
where walking the path
becomes a mantra.
Suddenly
a bright red leaf

falls before me,
amazing since it is
August 20th, but
then this is Vermont,
and the dew is heavy,
nights chilled,
like the wine last night
when we played cards
laughed and
might have held hands.

The Thinker

The next time
you're on the toilet
think about life.
Think about every other soul
sitting as well,
the poor, rich, famous,
everyone forced
to expel their lives.
Letting the air out of
their balloon, so to speak.

I think God is subtle
in a myriad of ways,
this being one—
saying to the smirk of ego,
your throne is made of waste.

Volume

for my Mother

When the sky is quiet,
then what space you held is quiet too.
The very place you stood
appears as if the clouds came
down in swirling winds,
and finger mist moves through my skin.

The sky in its solitude speaks
to all who stand and wait
in hope their endless search
for other bodies will not end,
as I search for one moment
that tells me you are near.

No amount of time can bring
the volume of your presence,
to feel it lean upon me even slightly.
I look upward in wonder
and wait for silver sprays of mint,
the smell of you to drop about me.

Midnight blue can ring itself
and stars will answer at the door.
If your weightless soul can press
the evening air, then I will wait among
the dust of those who trample lightly
my only claim to heaven's door.

Awakening

for Aaron

Early one evening at the hospital,
when my daughter had tired
from a sleepless cot vigil,
he nestled in my arms
ready for our nightly walk.
I told her sleep awhile.
You know he's safe with me.

So my grandson and I
walked and talked
to wall pictures,
    a water fountain,
      fire extinguisher,
    a telephone,
      stuffed animals,
to the windowed world.

His head slowly
plunked against my chest,
rising each time
another baby cried,
and soon I too craved quiet,
away from other small hearts.

We found it in an empty room,
whose four beds
stared as I
sat us on a wooden chair,

leaning back to
provide a warm chest bed.

He lay in undershirt and diaper.
I sat in a new world
where a small body
slowly rose and fell,
seeping in my heat
as my life went
beyond what I thought it was.

Princess Pine

for Giselle & Nick

On a narrow path,
one foot before the other,
the damp mush of mud wriggles
around and under exposed roots.

A bright green path of rounded moss,
its tipped sex organs glowing,
points on a fallen tree
to leaves and small growth blending.

Twenty yards ahead my friend's voice
echoes in this green temple,
where the snow cover of lichen
mingles with Partridge Berry.

We are hiking inside an emerald,
the great trees creating green air,
when there just to the side of the path
a lilliputian Princess Pine.

Falling to one knee I touch her skirt.

Typeset in Adobe Garamond
and ⲁDOBE GARAMOND EXPERT,
with titling in Linotype AG Frutiger 45 Light
and the book title in Adobe **LITHOS BOLD**,
and ornaments in Zapf Dingbats ✪
🌿 Adobe Woodtype,
on a Macintosh Quadra 610
and formatted
inQuarkXPress   4.1.